W9-API-756

DAY OF DESTINY
The Photographs of D-Day

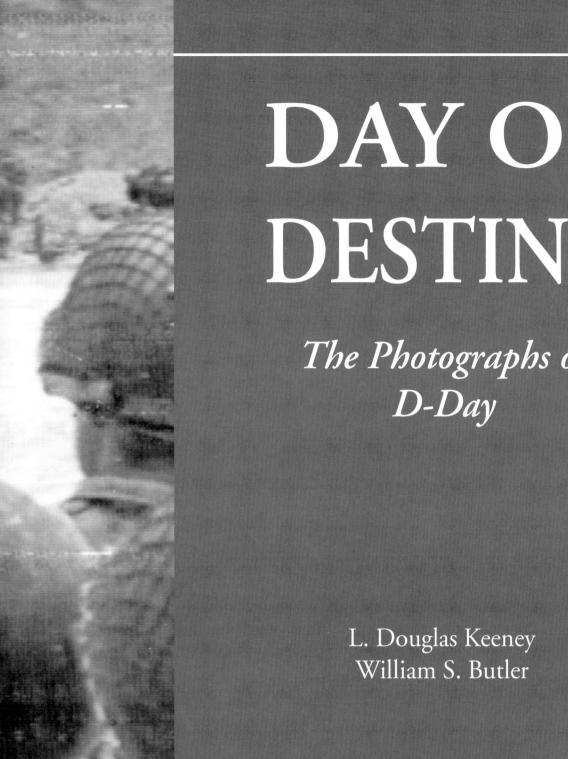

DAY OF DESTINY

The Photographs of D-Day

L. Douglas Keeney
William S. Butler

Quill
William Morrow
New York

These distinctive bands of black and white were applied to Allied aircaft during D-Day for quick identification. This pattern came to be known as "invasion stripes."

Copyright © 1998 by L. Douglas Keeney and William S. Butler

All rights reserved. No part of this book may be reproduced or utilized in any form or by any means, electronic or mechanical, including photocopying, recording, or by any information storage or retrieval system, without permission in writing from the Publisher. Inquiries should be addressed to Permissions Department, William Morrow and Company, Inc., 1350 Avenue of the Americas, New York, N.Y. 10019.

It is the policy of William Morrow and Company, Inc., and its imprints and affiliates, recognizing the importance of preserving what has been written, to print the books we publish on acid-free paper, and we exert our best effrorts to that end.

Robert Capa photos (pages 50-57) courtesy of Magnum Photos, Inc.

Library of Congress Cataloging-in-Publication Data has been applied for.

ISBN 0-688-16882-5

Printed in the United States of America

1 2 3 4 5 6 7 8 9 10

BOOK DESIGN BY AVION PARK

www.williammorrow.com

D-Day oral histories courtesy of The Eisenhower Center for American Studies,
Metropolitan College, University of New Orleans, and are reprinted with permission.

All photographs, except where indicated, are from the record groups of the
United States Coast Guard, the Army Signal Corps, the U.S. Navy and the U.S. Air Force
held at National Archives II, College Park, Maryland.

Many thanks:
Michael Murphy
Zach Schisgal
Jane O'Boyle
Mark Forman
Mike Morris

"Your enemy is well
trained, well equipped
and battle-hardened. He
will fight savagely."

"You are about to embark upon the Great Crusade, toward which we have striven these many months. The eyes of the world are upon you. The hopes and prayers of liberty-loving people everywhere march with you. In company with our brave Allies and brothers-in-arms on other Fronts, you will bring about the destruction of the German war machine, the elimination of Nazi tyranny over the oppressed peoples of Europe, and security for ourselves in a free world.

Your task will not be an easy one. Your enemy is well trained, well equipped, and battle-hardened. He will fight savagely.

But this is the year 1944. Much has happened since the Nazi triumphs of 1940-41. The united nations have inflicted upon the Germans great defeats, in open battle, man-to-man. Our air offensive has seriously reduced their strength in the air and their capacity to wage war on the ground. Our Home Fronts have given us an overwhelming superiority in weapons and munitions of war, and placed at our disposal great reserves of trained fighting men. The tide has turned! The free men of the world are marching together to Victory!

I have full confidence in your courage, devotion to duty and skill in battle. We will accept nothing less than full Victory!

Good Luck! And let us all beseech the blessing of Almighty God upon this great and noble undertaking."

—Gen. Dwight D. Eisenhower
June 5, 1944

CONTENTS

Nazi soldiers scramble for cover as an Allied reconnaissance aircraft swoops down to photograph the obstacles on the invasion beaches. At high tide these hazards were completely covered by water. The D-Day landing was scheduled at low tide in order to steer clear of these traps. At left, a German gun emplacement.

INTRODUCTION

On June 6, 1944, 150,000 Allied soldiers landed on five beaches in Normandy, in a bold attack on sixty divisions of tenacious, battle hardened German forces. The Allied troops would be the first to face 1.4 million of Hitler's best soldiers in France. By sheer numbers, the Normandy invasion was the greatest amphibious assault of all time. Five thousand ships, 11,000 aircraft, 175,000 troops in all. For sheer human determination and uncommon valor, D-Day remains the touchstone of modern military history.

After two years of planning, the Allied fleet of landing craft sailed into the teeth of the formidable German Atlantic Wall. Giant bunker fortresses with large artillery bore down murderously on the invaders. Thick smoke from mortar fire clouded the beaches. Heavy seas and incoming tides carried soldiers hundreds of yards off course, as they struggled to shore between deadly submerged mines and interlacing machine gun fire. At Omaha Beach, American troops were hit by artillery fire from 1,000 yards out in the water and across 200 yards of open beach.

Many units lost half their men even before reaching the seawalls and cliffs. For the first ninety minutes, an immeasurably long time on the bloody, bullet-ridden beaches, it looked as if Normandy would become an Allied defeat. But after continuous waves of incoming troops, one squad after the other silencing pillboxes and machine gun nests, the tide began to turn. Colonel George A. Taylor of the 16th Infantry Regiment recalled saying: "Two kinds of people are staying on this beach, the dead, and those about to die. Now let's get the hell out of here!" The American, Canadian and British soldiers who scaled the bluffs and stopped the German 88-millimeter guns often had no leaders, or orders—nothing beyond the simple fact that they were still alive.

Before the day ended there would be three thousand Allied casualties, and many more left uncounted, lost beneath the waves forever. For those who survived, there would be months of heated battle ahead before they achieved the liberation of Europe. But June 6 would remain forever the day that not only made history, but changed the future.

As military historians and authors, we were among the many people deeply moved by the first-person accounts of D-Day held at the Eisenhower Center at University of New Orleans, by the compelling narratives of the Center's Stephen Ambrose, and by Steven Spielberg's remarkably vivid film, "Saving Private Ryan." These works put the human face on an inhuman event and convey the personal experiences that made D-Day a living hell.

Not surprisingly, there are few photographs of the first wave of action on the beaches that day. Several combat photographers were killed on the invasion beaches, and servicemen who happened to have cameras certainly weren't in a position to use them. But, considering the circumstances, a remarkable number of incredible photographs were managed by brave combat journalists.

Their Normandy images have been located and compiled in this book. The moments they recall—the furtive smile of a nameless young soldier in a landing craft, bravely waiting for the ramp to open; a lifeless body on the rising surf; the wounded and shell-shocked survivors huddled close to the cliffs—will never fade from history's memory.

No collection of photographs can truly complete the portrait of blood, guts and glory on this small piece of coastline, many miles from home, half a century ago. This book is dedicated to the soldiers who never made it to the bluffs, and to the photographers, many of whose names we do not know. With this book, we hope to ensure no one ever forgets.

Above: Service on board an invasion vessel.
Overleaf: A formidable German observation
tower overlooking the invasion beaches awaits
the Allied invasion.

About The Photographs

The second assault wave hit Omaha Beach at 0700 and it also fared poorly. As had happened during the first wave, crossing bands of German automatic fire ripped through the landing craft as their ramps were lowered. American losses were again heavy and the prospect of surviving the exposed dash across the open sand seemed no better than it had before.

Into this fusillade came the boats of Company E of the 116th Infantry. Among the thirty young soldiers aboard was a press photographer, a veteran of conflict around the world, Robert Capa of *Life* Magazine. The very last to leave the landing craft, Capa leaped into the surf and began clicking away. He tucked in behind the crossed steel of a German beach obstacle and took pictures; he scurried to shoot more from the shelter of a burning tank, then made it to the seawall where he shot yet another roll.

Capa was on Omaha Beach for just minutes before suddenly dashing back out to a departing LCI. Safely aboard, he rushed to London where his precious film was developed. Sadly, complications in the developing room destroyed all but eight of his now famous images, most of which appear on these pages.

Capa was not the only journalist on the beaches. Ernest Hemingway came in on the seventh wave as a *Colliers* correspondent and Hollywood director John Ford brought in the cameras for the Offices of Strategic Services.

It was, however, the military itself that documented the entirety of D-Day. For all of the complexity of managing logistics during a war, much less an invasion as full of dangers as D-Day, all of the branches of the military deployed photographers to record the incredible events of June 6, 1944. The United States Navy and the Army Air Corps (which became the Air Force two years after the war) photographed their activities in support of the beach assaults, while the Army Signal Corps and the United States Coast Guard actually sent men ashore with the troops.

The collected images produced by these brave individuals now reside at the National Archives II in College Park, Maryland. Sixty plain gray boxes, each holding 100 or so black and white photographs, are silent witnesses to one of the most momentous days in world history.

L. Douglas Keeney   *William S. Butler*

MOUNTING THE INVASION

"The history of war
does not know
of an undertaking
comparable to it..."
—*Joseph Stalin*

Captain Callahan, our company commander, told us he had been to France and that it would be tough going. Hedgerows were built all over France. He told us that three out of four of us would not come back. He instructed us to kill everything that stood in the way of our going home. The soldiers were silent as each one of us tried to prepare for what lay ahead.

—*Warner Hamlett*

ENGLAND
JUNE 1944

After countless rehearsals, countless hours of boredom, and several false calls, the word came—this was it. D-Day was here. Now it was time to cross the channel and mount the invasion. But bad weather moved in on June 5th not only churning up the waves but also providing an ominous message about the battles ahead.

"Gear up!" was the cry as platoon leaders gathered their men and readied them for the voyage across the English Channel and into the teeth of Nazi Germany. In many ways, the soldiers who went into battle on D-Day were the best trained fighting force ever assembled to do battle. They were physically conditioned, they knew their mission objectives as well as they knew the backs of their hands and they expected the invasion to be difficult. This training, both physical and mental, would save many lives during the chaos of the landing. General Eisenhower (above right) made the final decision to go, but worried so much about it that he pre-wrote a note that he carried in his wallet notifying the President that the invasion had failed. Thankfully, Eisenhower never needed to send his brief message.

We deployed from Portsmouth, England on June 5, 1944. Late that night, we had a hot meal which was probably going to be our last one for quite a while. We got a few hours of sleep, and then at 0001 on D-Day, everyone was on the alert, curious and wondering exactly what to expect. We knew we had a long day ahead of us. All of the crew except me had been involved in other landings such as Italy and Southern France. I was probably the youngest man on board, and everybody was giving me words of encouragement. They were probably wondering how I would perform under fire, and I was wondering the same thing. We had no idea then that our landing area was Omaha Beach, nor that it was to be the bloodiest and heaviest of the German resistance in the entire invasion.

—Robert V. Miller

In each boat there were 30 men and the make-up was as follows: lieutenant, platoon sergeant, machine gunner with ammunition carrier, 60-millimeter mortar team, a flame-thrower, which Sgt. Robey had, a bazooka man, an ammo carrier, bangolore torpedoes for blowing barbed wire, pole charges, which was TNT on a pole, satchel charges, TNT done up in a burlap satchel. These were to be used on pillboxes. The rest of the personnel would be riflemen. The boats were flat bottomed with a ramp that dropped down in the front. They were known as LCIs. They were to carry one jeep or 30 men. We were to wear special jackets called assault jackets, rather than the full field pack and cartridge belt. The assault jackets had a lot of pockets and pouches in them. They contained rations for three days and a lot of ammunition. We wore a life belt under the jacket which was held together in the front with ties. If you were left off in deep water you were supposed to untie the jacket, slip out of it and inflate the life belt. We were also issued impregnated clothing in case the Germans used gas.

—Roger L. Brugger

Battleships, destroyers, landing ships tanks (LSTs), assault troop carriers and amphibious tracked vehicles (DUKWs) were among elements in the invasion flotilla seen here crossing the English Channel on D-Day. A B-26 Marauder passes the convoy overhead (right). Air support effectively blocked German fighters from joining the battle.

With invasion stripes painted under their wings, C-47s line up on the runway next to the troop-carrying gliders. The invasion plan called for airborne soldiers to be dropped behind the lines during the early hours of D-Day. Some would parachute in, others would be transported by gliders. Problems, however, abounded, not the least of which was that the Nazis booby-trapped open fields with stakes designed to rip apart man or glider. Elements of the 6th, 82nd and 101st went behind the lines and provided flanking cover for the invasion beaches.

The view the Germans had from a 77mm gun emplacement overlooking Omaha Beach.

Mine-tipped timber seen at high tide and low tide along the Normany coast. The invasion was set to begin during low tide to avoid the obstacles. Still, by early morning, the tide was in and boats fell to the German defenses.

Soldiers load into an LCVP, also known as a Higgins Boat, named for the designer. The Higgins Boats ferried back and forth from the big ships to the beach throughout the D-Day landings. The Coast Guard provided the pilots for the landings.

We were so overloaded with equipment that we could not board the plane without help. I carried an .03 rifle slung across my chest. The reason I had the .03 rifle was because Lieutenant Wendish had stated that one man had to have a grenade launcher, and we did not have grenade launchers that would fit the M-1 rifle. I also carried two Hawken mines, a bag of rifle grenades strapped to one leg, a gas mask strapped to the other, a trench knife strapped to my boots, another hung from my rifle belt along with wire cutters, entrenching shovel, bayonet, jump rope, and a canteen full of water. We also carried a musette bag with the usual full field equipment. This was also strapped to one leg. I had a belt full of .03 ammunition, and two extra bandoliers of the same, plus hand grenades. We wore a Mae West life preserver in case we went down in the Channel, and of course, the parachute on our backs plus a reserve chute on our chest.

—Sidney McCallum

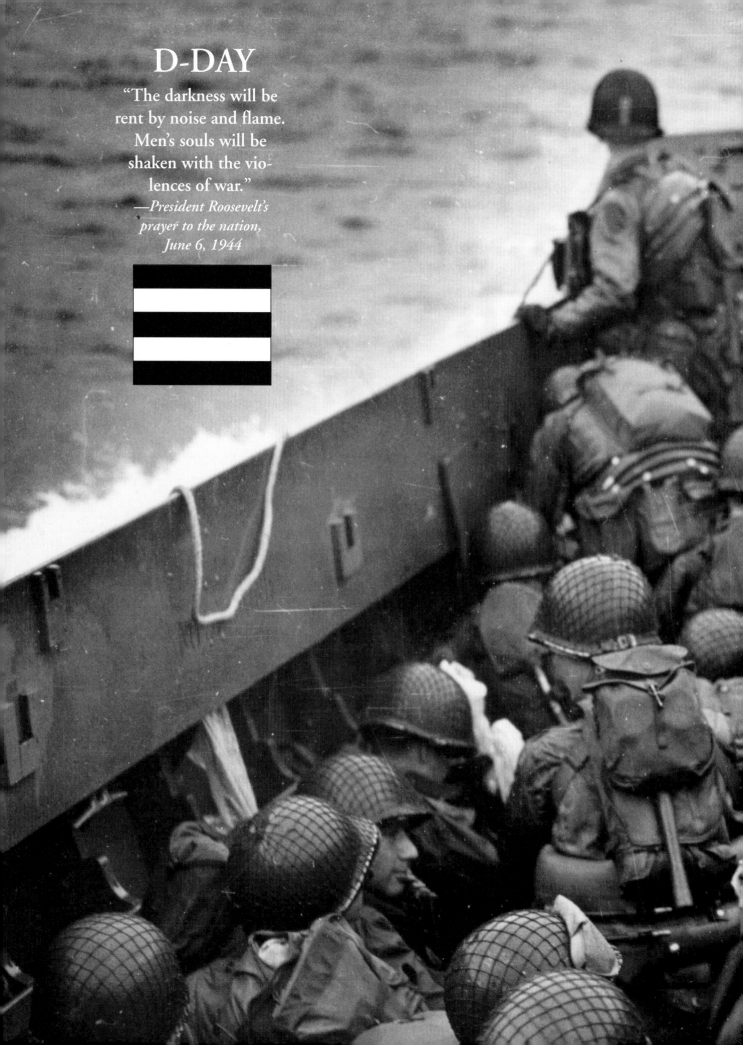

D-DAY

"The darkness will be
rent by noise and flame.
Men's souls will be
shaken with the vio-
lences of war."
—*President Roosevelt's
prayer to the nation,
June 6, 1944*

The battleship USS Nevada *softens up the invasion beaches with her 14-inch guns. Spent shell casings attest to the ferocity of the effort (bottom). Fire was suspended five minutes before the troops landed on the beaches. A 1000 yard safety line was established to protect the soldiers from the shelling when it commenced again.*

Anticipating the invasion, the Germans laid mines in all the likely attacking lanes to the beach. Here a U.S. mine sweeper explodes one just off Utah Beach.

This photo, taken at H-Hour on D-Day, shows German shells coming down on Army Rangers positioned on Iles Saint Marcouf just off Utah Beach.

Mines in the water, deadly artillery fire, mortar fire, machine gun nests and snipers with scopes all faced the assault craft and their cargo of soldiers as they approached the beaches.

The initial invasion force consisted of 34,142 men and 3,306 vehicles. Omaha Beach, a 7,000 yard section of beach midway between Caen and Carentan, was the main landing area.

(Right) Two Navy vessels stand by to pick up survivors as the minesweeper USS Tide (center) burns. Moments after this picture was taken, she sank beneath the surface. Notice that Navy censors have blotted out ship insignias.

Sergeant Barnes got shot down right in front of me, and Lieutenant Donaldson; Sergeant "Pilgrim"

Robertson, from my boat team, had a gaping wound in the upper right corner of his forehead.

He was walking crazily in the water, without his helmet. Then I saw him get down on his knees

and start praying with his rosary beads. At this moment, the Germans cut him in half with their

deadly crossfire, which was coming from pillboxes, and what I thought was a reinforced building

overlooking the beach. I saw the reflection from the helmet of one of the snipers and took

aim and later on, I found out, I got a bull's eye on him. It was my only time that rifle fired,

due to the bullet that hit my rifle. It must have shattered the wood, and the rifle broke in

half and I had to throw it away.

—Harold Baumgarten, M.D.

"Belgian hedgehogs," five-foot-high crossed beams of welded railway ties, were designed to stave in the bottoms of the attack boats. At low tide, they provided soldiers with some cover, albeit scant, from the probing machine gun and mortar fire.

Attacking at low tide meant the landing craft pilots could see the obstructions in the water, but it left them further off-shore, increasing the distance the soldiers had to sprint before they reached the cover of the seawalls or cliffs.

I remember floundering in the water with my hand up in the air, I guess I was trying to get my balance, when I was first shot. I was shot through the palm of my hand. Next to me, in the water, a fellow was rolling over towards me. I remember him very clearly saying, "Sergeant, they're leaving us here to die like rats." At any rate, I made my way forward but I was hit several times, once in the left thigh, which broke a hip bone. I remember being hit in the pack a couple of times, feeling a tug on my chin strap on my helmet which was severed by a bullet. I worked my way up against the wall and sort of collapsed there.

—*Thomas Valance*

*Tracked vehicles came in with the first wave and their remains provided some
cover to troops of the second wave, seen here. Note the curving exhaust stacks.
These vehicles were "waterproofed" to help them get through the surf. Not able to
clearly see the enemy firing positions, soldiers advanced purely on instinct.*

The tide was coming in and our beach was getting smaller. We could see the bodies of the dead rolling in the surf. Our company commander took a shrapnel wound to his left leg that was so severe, the medic couldn't stop the bleeding and he bled to death. The company executive officer, second in command, took over and he had the company for less than an hour when a sniper got him. We only lost one man in our boat group; he got hit in the shoulder. The Germans were using wooden bullets and they made a very nasty wound. After what seemed like an eternity, we started up the draw to the top of the cliff overlooking the beach. We

had just got a good start up the draw when we were pinned down by a machine gun emplacement built in to the side of the cliff. By radio, the Navy was contacted and a destroyer came in quite close to the beach and stopped dead in the water. A sailor came out of the hatch and went to a forward gun turret, turned the gun towards the machine gun emplacement and let go with a couple of rounds. This silenced the machine gun.

—*Roger L. Brugger*

As dawn broke, we were enveloped in smoke from dust and shell bursts. Landing craft armed with 4.7-inch guns, and others fitted with large rocket launchers, began bombarding the sandy beach and the dunes beyond. While we were en route to the landing area, a terrific explosion occurred to my right, which turned out to be an explosion of an LCT hitting a sea mine. Only three people survived.

—*John L. Ahearn*

Both the seawall on Omaha Beach (above) and the cliffs at Utah Beach (right) provided comparative shelter to the advancing troops. In the first waves, soldiers were often without their weapons and leaderless by the time they got through the surf and across the sand, but they were happy to be alive.

Later, as the German fire began to let up, we began an evacuation. A couple of LCM Higgins Boats came in as close as they could without being grounded themselves. We managed to get the wounded men on some of our litters and over the side with the help of the non-wounded crewmen, and we put them on the LCMs and we had quite a ways to wade out to the boats and the Germans were still trying to reach us with their machine gun fire. The LCMs took us to a destroyer, U.S.S. *Doyle*, where Mudgett and I assisted the ship's doctor to dress the wounds in their main battle dressing station, the officer's ward room. One of the destroyer sailors gave me a set of dungarees to replace my bloody mess of coveralls.

—*Robert V. Miller*

The Army Rangers faced the near vertical bluffs at Pointe du Hoc. Their mission was to scale these cliffs and drive inland to destroy the Germans' deadly 155mm artillery batteries. Two divisions faced this rocky, 85 foot cliff, assaulting it with climbing ropes and sheer willpower. Above and right: Soldiers rest and tend to the wounded at the base of the cliffs.

Left: LCTs in the background transported the wounded back to the assault ships as soon as they offloaded their vehicles. A steady stream of new soldiers (right) landed for days, setting up rallying points among the rocky hills (bottom right) and organizing for the inland push.

(Above) Using a steel cable, these men have rigged a lifeline for soldiers having trouble in the surf. (Below) Grim-faced survivors from a deadly shelling that destroyed their landing craft make it to the shore on Omaha Beach after paddling across hundreds of yards of open water. (Right) Coast Guardsmen rescue survivors from a sunken landing craft.

The ramp goes down and I'm the first guy shot, machine gunned through the right side. When I stepped out, I stepped into water over my head. The guys from my platoon pulled me out, and I just rushed to the base of the cliff and grabbed any rope and up the cliff we went. We rushed as quickly as we could to our three gun emplacements, our objectives. There were snipers around and machine guns firing at us. We played it like we play a football game. Charging hard and low.

—Leonard Lomell

When we got near the top of the cliff, I talked to Sergeant England who had been injured also. He told me I was pale, and I showed him my leg that was now swelling and turning different colors. My spine was sending jabbing pains through my body. Sergeant England told me to go back to the beach and get a medic to tag me so that I could be transported back to the big ship. The two of us returned to the beach. Thousands of bodies lined it. You could walk on the bodies, as far as you could see along the beach, without touching the ground. Parts of bodies floated, heads, arms, legs—and I stepped gently. Medics walked up and down the beach tagging the wounded. I realized now what being in the first wave was all about.

—Warner Hamlett

Smooth glider landings in the rough farm fields were almost impossible, particularly at night. Nonetheless, these gliders (top) were actually disassembled to facilitate unloading, not torn apart as so many others were as they touched down. (Bottom) A U.S. casualty of the pre-dawn landings.

We could hear the sounds of planes in the distance, then no sounds at all. This was followed by a series of swishing noises followed by a loud crash and intermittent screams. The gliders were coming in rapidly, one after the other, from all directions. Many overshot the field and landed in the surrounding woods while others crashed into the nearby farmhouses and stone walls. In a moment, the field was complete chaos. Bodies and bundles were thrown all along the length of the field. Some of the glider troopers were impaled by the splintering wood of the fragile machines.

—John Fitzgerald

Below: After landing their gliders behind enemy lines, Army pilots were told to make their way forward to the beaches, disrupting communication lines wherever possible along the way. From the beaches, they were returned to England and given new planes to fly.

Belinski and I sat there all that day looking at the war. We got a real good look at all the landings that were taking place. We watched the troops come down the causeway, then came the 12th Infantry and the 22nd, then later in the afternoon the 90th Division began to show up. There were a lot of planes going over, a lot of P-47s checking the beaches. I remember that there were several German planes that flew over and really got the ack-ack guns going at them.

—*Joseph S. Blaylock, Sr.*

British soldiers in American vehicles head toward Utah Beach.

Right: A French tank rolls off an LST and on to Normandy.

The sky was full of airplanes, and below, the water was covered with streams of surface vessels. At this altitude, the assault forces were in full view. We kept expecting to see German fighters as we neared the coast but so far so good. We had heard all along that we had mostly destroyed their air power. We believed we were right. Out over the French countryside, scattered everywhere, were parachutes and patches of huge crashed gliders. We had a sickening feeling that things were not going so well.

—James M. DeLong

Omaha Beach and Utah Beach became the main points of entry for supplies and troops advancing inland. These troops were among those which found themselves in the Battle of the Bulge in December.

(Above and right, top) Steel reinforced bunkers such as these, part of Hitler's much vaunted Atlantic Wall, easily withstood the pounding by Allied shells and bombs. For the men inside, however, the concussions were debilitating. (Below) An elaborate system of trenches was built by the Germans to connect living quarters with their gun emplacements and ammunition storage areas.

This is what the D-Day beaches looked like after the assaults. B-17, B-24 and B-26 bombers tried to place their bombs to blow shell craters, such as the one being examined above, for the troops to use as foxholes.

These skirted tanks were designed to maneuver through water much like an amphibious truck. While the inflation bags tested well in exercises before the invasion, in practice they proved to be more vulnerable than they looked. Scores of these tanks rolled off their LSTs only to founder and sink in the rough water. Nonetheless, the tankers opened fire almost as the ramps opened and continued blazing away even as they went under.

German Panzer tanks were the best armored vehicles made at the time, and the young men who manned them were considered among the Wehrmacht elite. But gasoline supplies, thanks to Allied bombing, were low, limiting their mobility. American tank destroyers (above) arrived in force after D-Day, and set about the destruction of the Panzer divisions. Tank battles between American-built Shermans and Panzers continued well into 1945, when overwhelming numbers eventually gave the Americans the upper hand.

I began moving our six tanks southward on the beach as it became apparent that Exit 2 was jammed as others tried to get through the sea wall. I spotted a narrow opening that had been used by enemy vehicles. I instructed my tank driver to "gun it" and we sped through the opening. As soon as we got through we turned left and discovered a large fortification between the seawall and the road. I called for our tanks to fire. Within seconds of our hits, a number of soldiers came out waving a white cloth.

—*John L. Ahearn*

Many of the soldiers Hitler threw into the defense of France were just young boys, conscripted to replace depleted forces. Here an American GI asks a young soldier to present his papers.

Paratroopers display their first souvenir of the war.

Even before the beaches were lost, German soldiers were surrendering to the squads advancing inland. The Allied soldiers, not wanting to deal with prisoners who would only slow their progress, told the Nazis to march to the beach and surrender to the first American they saw. This is what it looked like on D-Day.

(Left) This remarkable panorama shows the contrast between the quiet French countryside and the hell that was the invasion beaches. (Above) Night falls on D-Day and German night attack aircraft swoop in to bomb the fleet. A seemingly impenetrable wall of tracers go up to meet the bombers but already a transport, foreground, has been hit and is sinking stern first.

BUILDING
THE
BEACHHEAD

(Below and facing page) After the invasion itself was over, the military turned to the dull, repetitive business of logistics. Navy Seabees and the engineers turned the sand into a true port and the flow of men and material was almost constant. Altogether, 156,000 people landed on the beaches.

After being used to land invasion forces, the gliders became mini-freighters. Seen below crossing the invasion beaches, these gliders will resupply the advancing soldiers.

In addition to the roughly 50,000 men landed on Omaha Beach, 17,000 more were preloaded for landings on D+1 and D+2. Thirty-two thousand more soldiers (and 9,400 vehicles) were scheduled to arrive between D+3 and D+15. The appearance of calm in many of these pictures is an illusion; enemy shells were a constant threat for days after the initial assault.

108

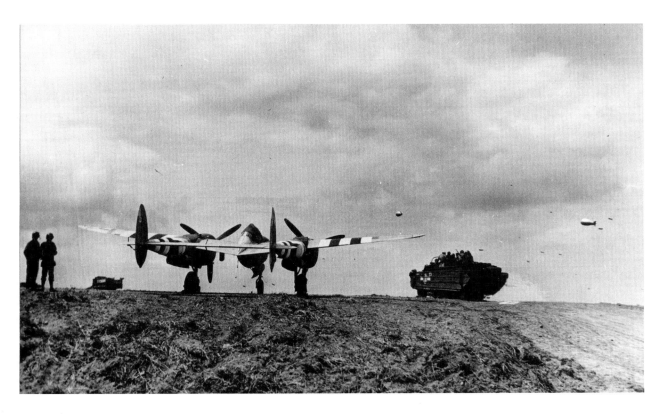

Air power played several important roles during and after D-Day. (Left) Two B-24 bombers are joined by a pair of P-47 Thunderbolt fighters as they sortie over the invasion beaches. Bombing softened up the German defenses and then served to hinder the flow of reinforcements to the invasion area. (Bottom Left) This P-38 stands on a hastily built airstrip overlooking the beaches. The fighters provided high air cover protection against the German Luftwaffe and then began low level strafing.

(Below) The C-47 was a true workhorse of the sky. Seen here pulling gliders inland, the C-47 entered civilian service as the popular DC-3.

The price of victory was staggering. The bloodiest moment of the invasion was the morning of June 6, and most of the casualties occurred in the first two hours. On Omaha Beach alone 2,400 men were killed, wounded or reported as missing in action. Altogether, the Allies counted about 10,000 men as killed, wounded or missing in action during Operation Overlord.

A medic lights a smoke for an injured soldier.

A chaplain administers rites for fallen paratroopers, killed in the bloody action in the pre-dawn hours of D-Day.

MOVING
INLAND

(Above) Paratroopers relax momentarily in a small French town. (Right) With dead cattle ignored as just another consequence of war, soldiers carry on with the planning necessary to advance.

(Facing page, bottom) For many, these inflatable belts were lifesavers. Then they were merely trash along the roadside, discarded as soldiers advanced inland.

(Below) A German sniper comes under fire as soldiers direct their antitank weapons toward the farmhouse that conceals him.

After the battalion had landed, Jack and I moved out and saw someone approaching us, so I gave the password, "Flash," and he did not answer. I gave it again and *still* got no answer, so I decided to shoot, but before I pulled the trigger, he gave the countersign, "Thunder." This person was Corporal Winn, our medic. Corporal Winn may have used his cricket, an American toy usually gotten in Cracker Jacks, but if he did, I did not hear it, and would not have known what it was—as I did not receive one—nor was I informed that they were to be used as a signaling device.

—*Sidney McCallum*

Shaving in the first mirror they could find, two soldiers clean up next to a French farmhouse.

American paratroopers get a few moments of rest before resuming their pursuit of retreating German forces.

The events of June 6, 1944 seem like an unending nightmare.

But I would do it all over again to stop someone like Hitler.

—*Warner Hamlett*

(Above and facing page) This is General Dwight D. Eisenhower. He was loved by his soldiers, respected as the Supreme Commander Allied Expeditionary Force—and greatly relieved that the invasion was a success. He and General Omar Bradley, right, quietly acknowledge the happiness they feel.

June 6, 1944. When it was all over, a battle-weary GI received the thanks of a grateful French citizen.